One Hundred Flowers

1 *Red Poppy*, 1927

A flower is relatively small. Everyone has many associations with a flower – the idea of flowers. You put out your hand to touch the flower – lean forward to smell it – maybe touch it with your lips almost without thinking – or give it to someone to please them. Still – in a way – nobody sees a flower – really – it is so small – we haven't time – and to see takes time like to have a friend takes time. If I could paint the flower exactly as I see it no one would see what I see because I would paint it small like the flower is small.

So I said to myself – I'll paint what I see – what the flower is to me but I'll paint it big and they will be surprised into taking time to look at it –

Georgia O'Keeffe
"About Myself," 1939

Georgia O'Keeffe

One Hundred Flowers

Edited by Nicholas Callaway

Alfred A. Knopf

in association with Callaway · New York · 1989

This is a Borzoi Book
Published by Alfred A. Knopf, Inc.
Copyright © 1987 by Callaway Editions, Inc.
All rights reserved under International and Pan-American Copyright Conventions.
Published in the United States by Alfred A. Knopf, Inc., 201 East 50th Street, New York, NY, 10022
in association with Callaway Editions, Inc., 54 Seventh Avenue South, New York, NY 10014
and simultaneously in Canada by Random House of Canada Limited, Toronto. Distributed by Random House, Inc., New York.

Library of Congress Cataloging-in-Publication Data

O'Keeffe, Georgia, 1887–1986
Georgia O'Keeffe: One Hundred Flowers

1. O'Keeffe, Georgia, 1887–1986.   2. Flowers in art.   3. Painting, American.   4. Painting, Modern—20th century—United States.
I. Callaway, Nicholas.   II. Title.   III. Title: Georgia O'Keeffe: One Hundred Flowers.
ND237.05A4   1987   759.13   87-2842
ISBN 0-679-72408-7
ISBN 0-394-56218-6 (hc.)

The statement by Georgia O'Keeffe that follows Plate 1 is excerpted from a text entitled "About Myself,"
published in the catalogue accompanying her 1939 exhibition at An American Place, New York.

Front Jacket: *Jimson Weed*, 1932. Oil on canvas, 48 x 40 inches (121.9 x 101.6 cm). Estate of Anita O'Keeffe Young. (Plate 96).
Back Jacket: *Red Poppy*, 1927. Oil on canvas, 7⅛ x 9 inches (18.1 x 22.9 cm). Private Collection. (Plate 1).
Inside Front Jacket: *Calla Lilies*, 1923. Oil on canvas, 32 x 12 inches (81.3 x 30.5 cm). Private Collection. (Plate 50).
Inside Back Jacket: *Iris*, 1929 (also entitled *Dark Iris No. 2*, 1927).
Oil on canvas, 32 x 12 inches (81.3 x 30.5 cm). Colorado Springs Fine Arts Center, Anonymous Gift. (Plate 32).
Frontispiece: *Black Iris*, 1926 [*The Dark Iris No. III*, 1926]. Oil on canvas, 36 x 29⅞ inches (91.4 x 75.9 cm).
The Metropolitan Museum of Art. Alfred Stieglitz Collection, 1969. Courtesy Estate of Georgia O'Keeffe. (Plate 2).
Facing Page: *Georgia O'Keeffe*, Lake George, 1918. Photograph by Alfred Stieglitz.
Silver chloride print, 3⁹⁄₁₆ x 4⁹⁄₁₆ inches (9 x 11.6 cm). Courtesy of Gilman Paper Company Collection.
Last Page: *Georgia O'Keeffe*, Abiquiu, New Mexico, c. 1951. Photograph by Doris Bry.
Gelatin silver print, 6¹¹⁄₁₆ x 4¾ inches (17 x 12.1 cm). Copyright © 1987 Doris Bry.

Callaway Editions specializes in the design, production, and publication of illustrated books.
Their titles include *Alfred Stieglitz: Photographs and Writings*; *Still Life: Hollywood Tableaux Photographs*;
Eiko by Eiko and *Issey Miyake: Photographs by Irving Penn*.

Printed and bound in Japan
First Edition, 1987
First Paperback Edition, 1989

Georgia O'Keeffe, Lake George, 1918. Photograph by Alfred Stieglitz

3 *Red Canna,* c. 1919

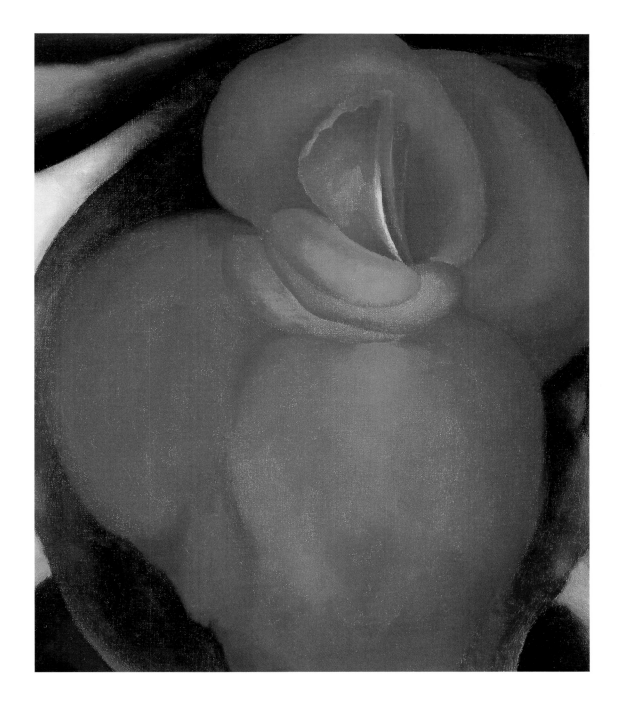

4 *Red Flower*, c. 1918–1919

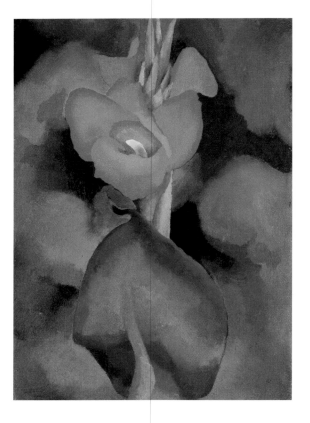

5 *Red Canna*, 1919

6 *Red Canna*, c. 1919

7 *Inside Red Canna*, 1919

8 *Zinnias*, c. 1920

9 [*Still Life–Zinnias*], c. 1920

10 *Red Canna*, 1923

11 *Red Snapdragons*, c. 1923

14 *Flower Abstraction*, 1924

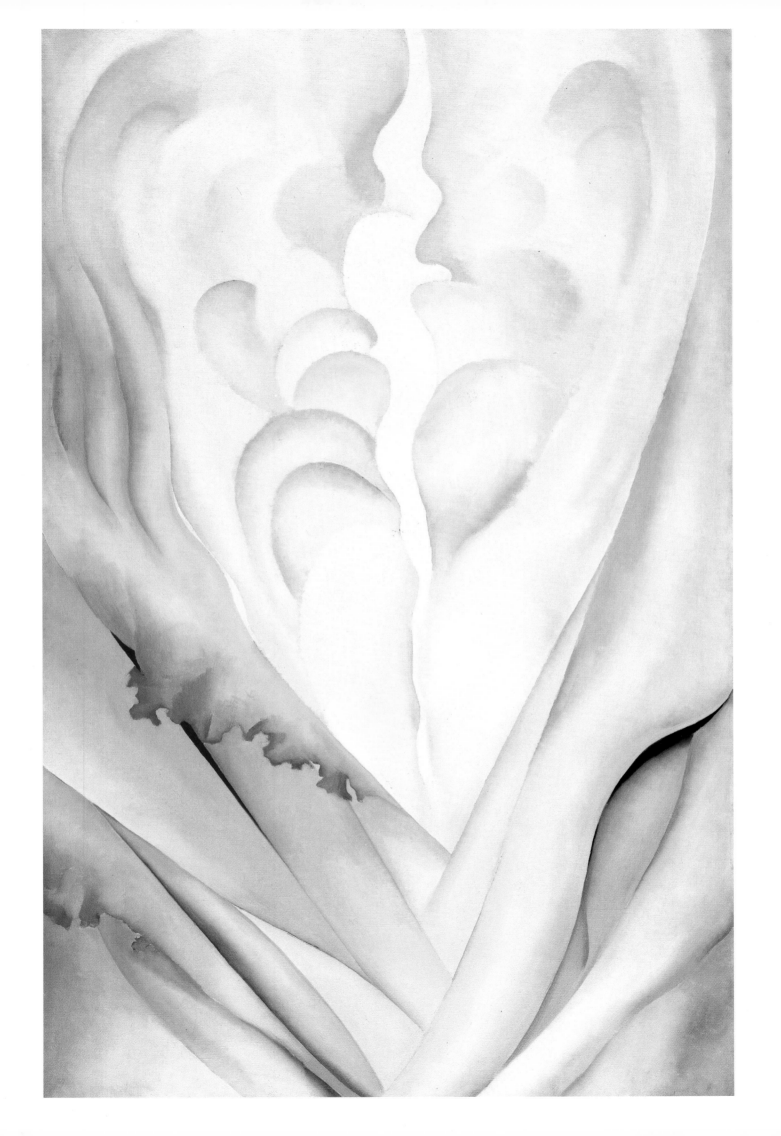

16 *Purple Petunia,* c. 1925

17 *Red Canna*, 1925

18 *Petunia, Lake George,* 1925   19 *Petunia,* 1925

20 *Purple Petunias*, 1925

21 *Petunia*, 1925

22 *Bleeding-Heart*, c. 1928   23 *Blue Flower*, 1924–28

24 *Yellow Sweet Peas*, 1925

25 *White Sweet Peas*, 1926

26 *Pink Sweet Peas, 1927*

27 *Purple Petunia,* 1927

28 *Abstraction–77*, 1925 [*Pink Tulip*, 1925]

29 *Pink Tulip*, 1926

30 *Black and Purple Petunias*, 1925

31 *White Iris*, c. 1926   32 *Iris*, 1929 [*Dark Iris No. 2*, 1927]

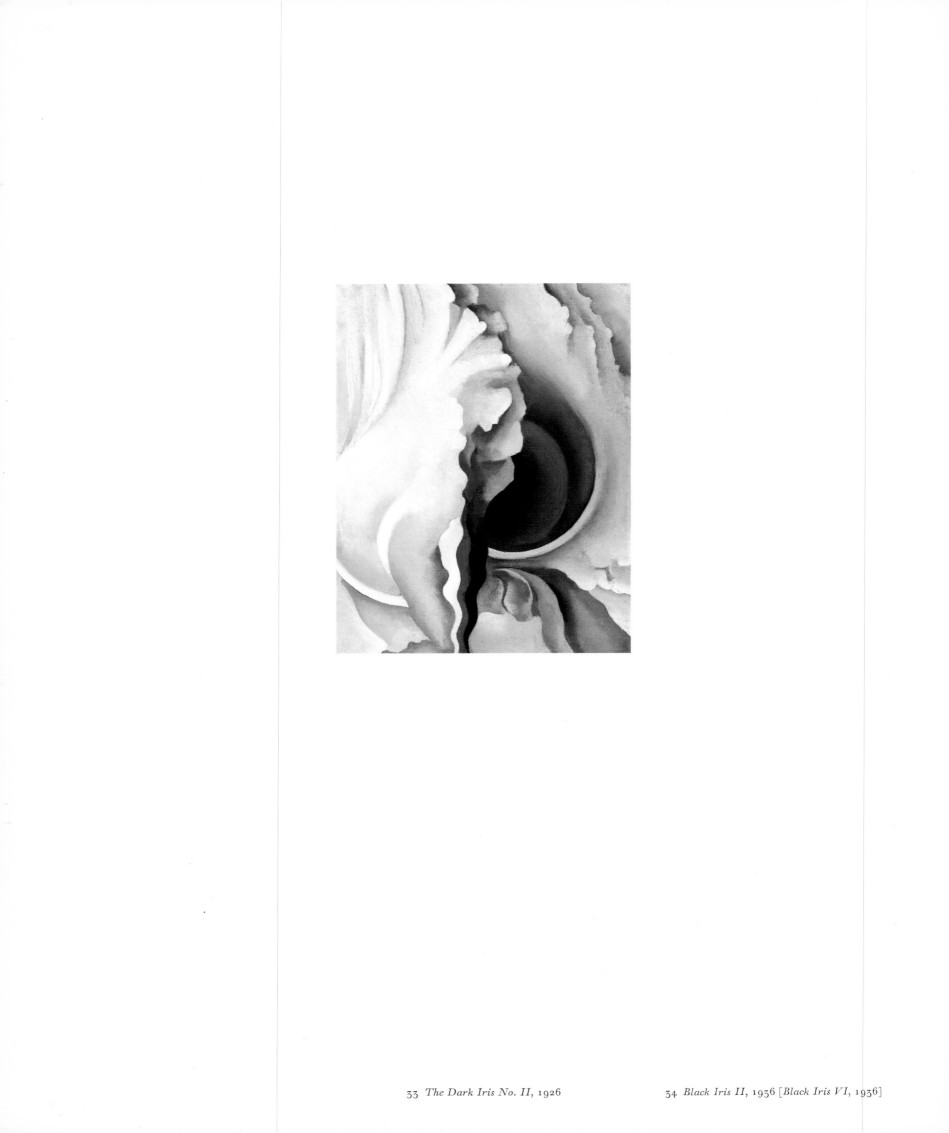

33 *The Dark Iris No. II*, 1926   34 *Black Iris II*, 1936 [*Black Iris VI*, 1936]

35 *Pansy*, 1926 [*Black Pansy & Forget-Me-Nots*, 1926]

36 *Nicotina* [Nicotiana], c. 1926 [*Autumn Leaf and White Flower*, c. 1926]

41 *Abstraction–White Rose No. 3*, 1927 [*Ballet Skirt* or *Electric Light*, 1927]

42 *White Rose with Larkspur No. 1*, 1927

43 *White Rose with Larkspur No. 2, 1927*

44 *White Pansy*, 1927 [*Pansy with Forget-Me-Nots*, 1927]

46 *Poppy*, 1927

47 *Single Lily with Red*, 1928 [*Calla Lily on Red*, 1928]

48 *Calla Lily with Red Background*, 1923   49 *Calla Lily*, 1923

50 *Calla Lilies*, 1923

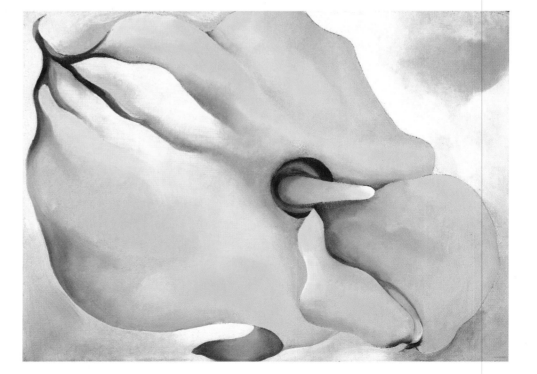

51 *Lily–Yellow No. 2,* 1927   52 *Yellow Calla,* 1926

53 *Yellow Calla–Green Leaves*, 1927 [*Lily–Yellow No. 1*, 1927]

54 *Calla Lily on Grey*, 1928

preceding pages:

55 *Calla Lily with Red Roses, 1926 [L.K.–White Calla & Roses, 1926]*

56 *Calla Lilies with Red Anemone, 1928*

57 *Two Calla Lilies on Pink, 1928*

58 *Pink Rose, 1928*

59 *White Rose,* 1928 [*A Rose on Blue,* 1928]

60 *Jack-in-the-Pulpit No. 1*, 1930

61 *Yellow Hickory Leaves with Daisy*, 1928

preceding pages:

62 *Jack-in-the-Pulpit No. 2*, 1930

63 *Jack-in-the-Pulpit No. 3*, 1930

64 *Jack-in-the-Pulpit No. 4*, 1930

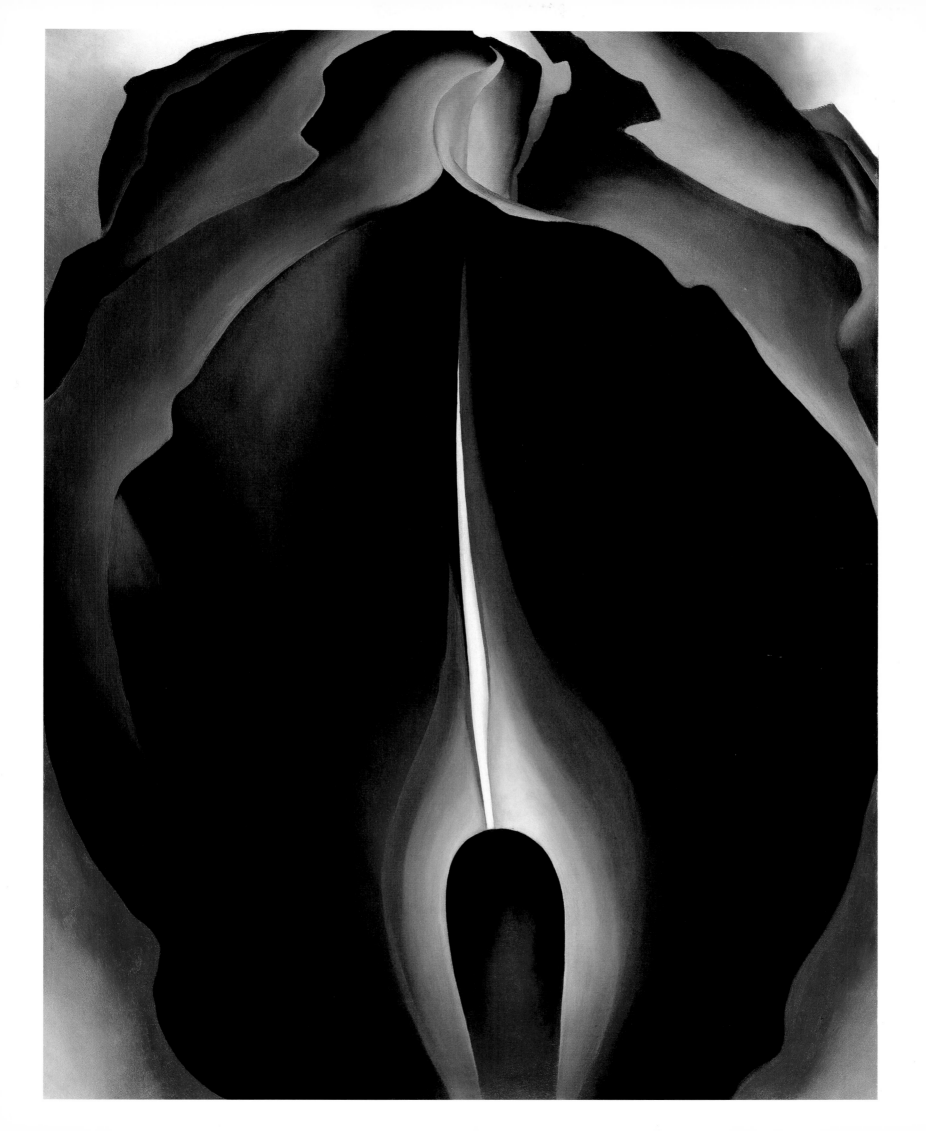

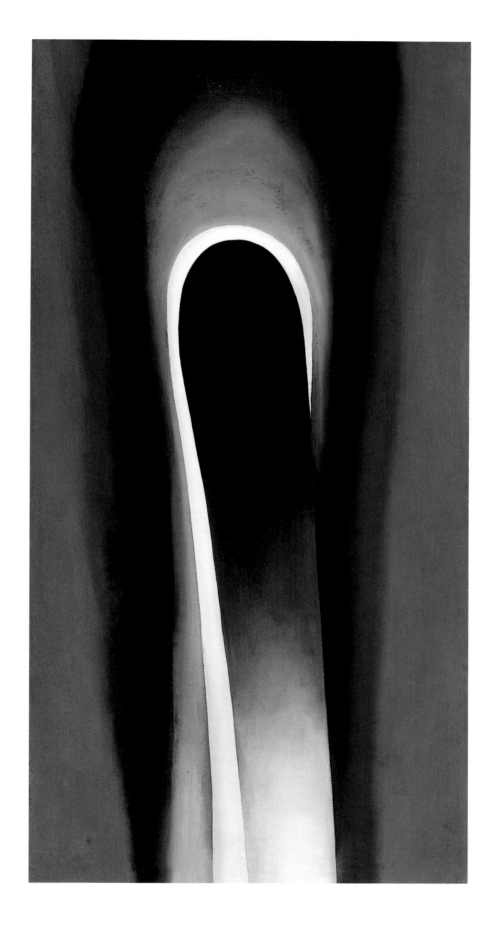

66 *Jack-in-the-Pulpit No. 6*, 1930

67 *White Flower*, 1929

69 *Black Hollyhock, Blue Larkspur*, 1929

70 *Black Hollyhock, Blue Larkspur,* 1929

preceding pages:

71 *Oriental Poppies*, 1928 [*Red Poppies*, 1928]

72 *Yellow Cactus Flowers*, 1929

73 *Light Iris*, 1930 [*White Iris*, 1930]

74 *Banana Flower No. 1*, 1933

75 *Banana Plant No. 4*, 1933

76 *Banana Flower*, 1933

77 *Banana Flower*, 1933

78 *Calla Lilies, 1930*

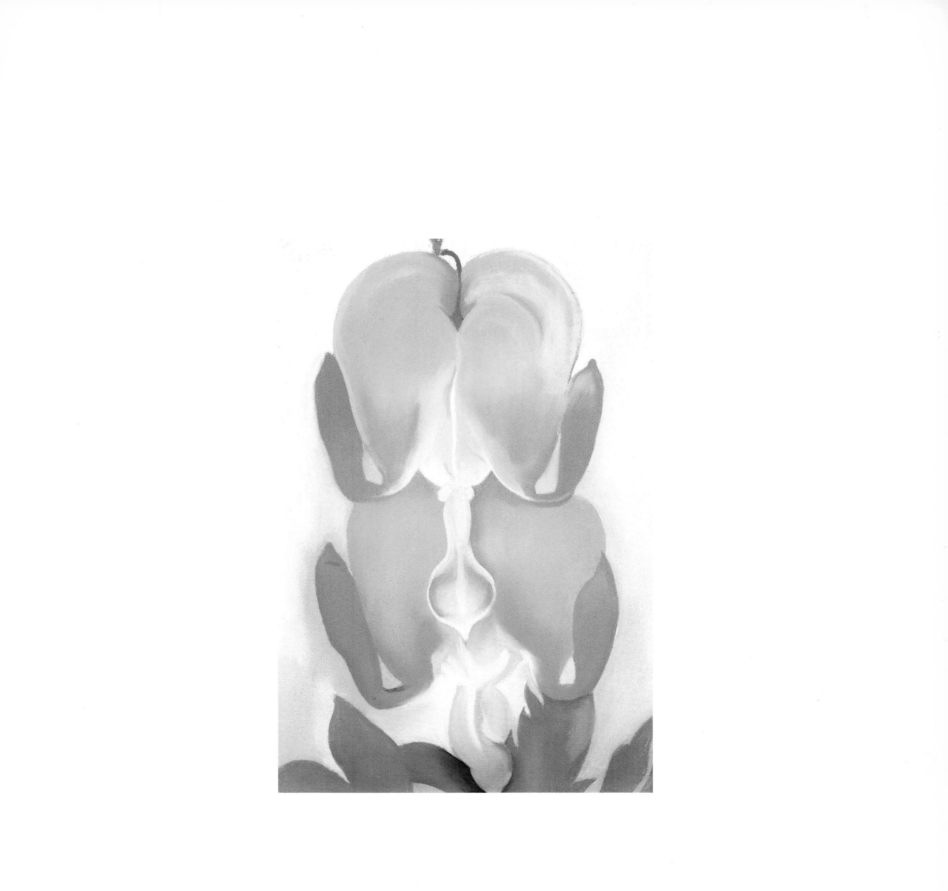

79 *Bleeding-Heart*, 1932

81 *Pink Roses and Larkspur, 1931*

82 *Lilac, Carnation, Tulip, 1938 [Flowers, 1941]*   83 *Apple Blossoms, 1930*

84 *Red Amaryllis*, 1937

87 *Cup of Silver*, 1939

89 *The Miracle Flower*, 1936

90 *White Primrose,* 1947

91 *White Flower on Red Earth No. 1*, 1943

92 *Narcissa's Last Orchid*, 1941

93 *White Camellia*, 1938

94 *An Orchid*, 1941

96 *Jimson Weed*, 1932

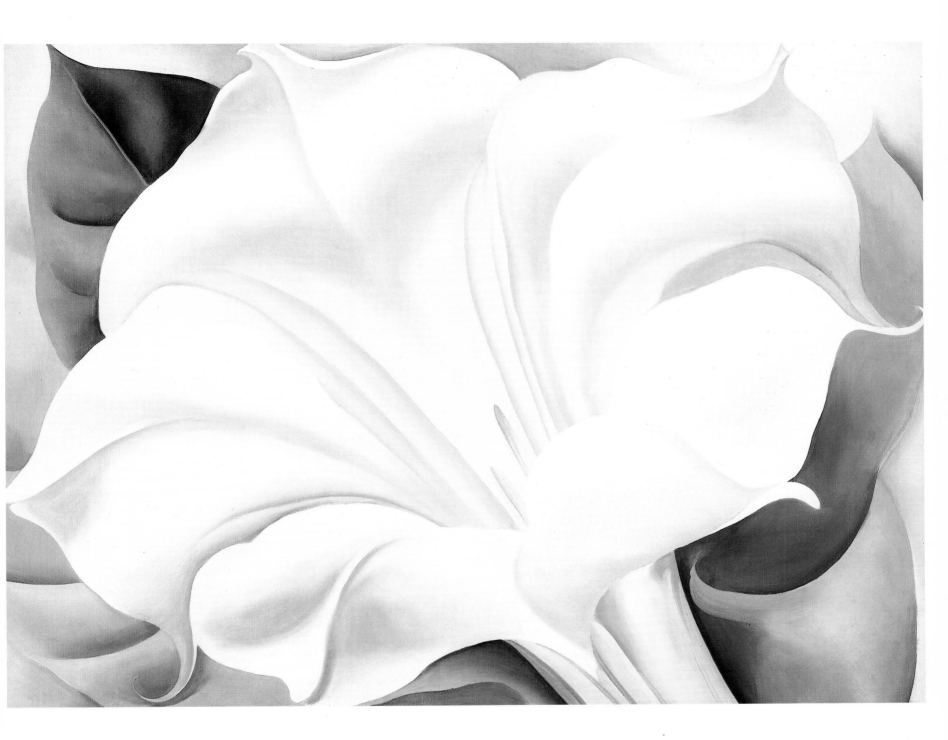

97 *The White Trumpet Flower, 1932*

98 *The White Calico Flower, 1931*

99 *White Rose, New Mexico, 1930*

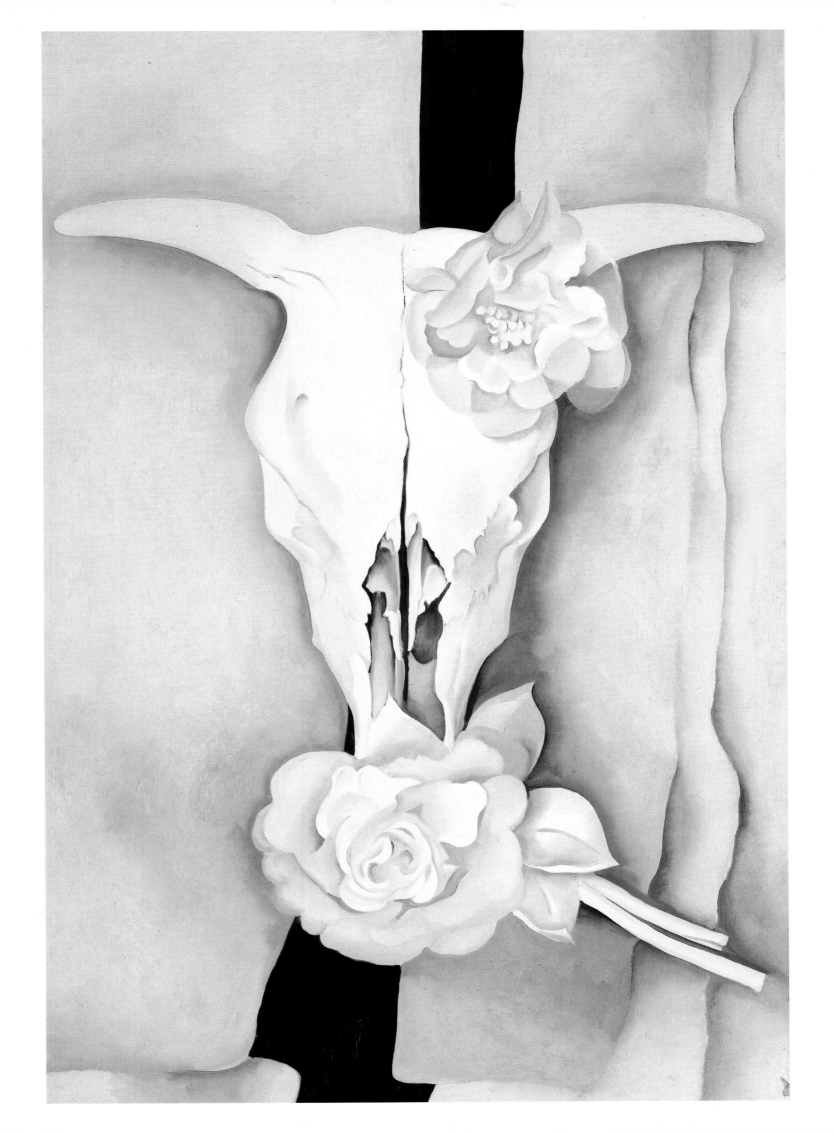

Afterword

Georgia O'Keeffe was not a flower painter. She may be, however, the greatest painter of flowers in the history of Western art. She always stressed the primacy of the artist's vision over subject matter, and staunchly resisted those who would categorize her works by genre, school, or gender.

It would be incorrect to assess O'Keeffe's contribution to twentieth century American art on the basis of the flower paintings alone. In her exhibitions and books, she took care to ensure that all of her themes—abstractions, desert landscapes, city views, bones, shells, flowers, and other natural forms—be seen in relation to each other. Nevertheless, it is important to look at this body of work as a whole, because it occupied a place in O'Keeffe's life and art that is distinct and distinctive.

By the end of her ninety-eight years, she had made over two hundred flower paintings, the majority produced in a period of extraordinary and sustained creativity that lasted from 1918 to 1932. When O'Keeffe began to paint flowers she was a young woman of thirty, and very much in love with Alfred Stieglitz, a world-renowned photographer. They had met in 1916 when Stieglitz first exhibited her work in New York at his gallery *291*, the center of avant-garde art in America. Here he showed in 1916 and 1917 the landmark group of purely abstract drawings and watercolors O'Keeffe had completed on her own while teaching in South Carolina and Texas. Their life together in New York began in 1918. In the summer of 1923, Stieglitz mounted an exhibition of one hundred oils, drawings, and watercolors by O'Keeffe that included her first small flower paintings. The first large-scale canvases were completed in 1924, the year of their marriage, and were shown in 1925 at the "Seven Americans" exhibition held by Stieglitz at the Anderson Galleries.

When these giant flowers were exhibited, they caused a sensation, eliciting a host of reactions ranging from critical raves to outrage to awe. One reviewer said that confronting an O'Keeffe flower painting tends to make the viewer feel "as if we humans were butterflies."[1] Even Stieglitz's first reaction to them was equivocal; when O'Keeffe called him into her studio to show him *Petunia No. 2*, 1924 (Plate 12), his first response was: "Well, Georgia, I don't know how you're going to get away with anything like that—you aren't planning to show it, are you?"[2]

A number of things about these paintings stunned viewers. The first was their physical size in relation to the actual dimensions of the subject. O'Keeffe took an object that in reality might be only an inch or so tall and enlarged it, sometimes up to 48 inches high. The largest was the 6 x 7 foot *Miracle Flower* from 1936 (Plate 89). (It is interesting, though, that even O'Keeffe's tiny 7 x 9 inch oils, like Plates 1 and 33, often have the same monumentality.) Most often the blossom was shown in extreme close-up and in minute detail. The combination of size and scale was overwhelming. In 1938, James W. Lane wrote in *Apollo* magazine, "The observer feels like Alice after she had imbibed the 'Drink Me' phial." Another writer imagined these colossal flowers as a "boutonnière for Gargantua."[3]

O'Keeffe was aiming for this impact, as she explained in a 1946 interview in the *New York Post*:

> *"When you take a flower in your hand and really look at it,"* she said,
> *cupping her hand and holding it close to her face, "it's your world for the*
> *moment. I want to give that world to someone else. Most people in the city*
> *rush around so, they have no time to look at a flower. I want them to see it*
> *whether they want to or not."*[4]

O'Keeffe's palette was as startling as the gigantic scale of her canvases. No American painter had explored such radical combinations of color nor such astonishing intensity of hue. The colors favored at that time by her contemporaries and colleagues were for the most part "dreary," as she called them—somber and low-toned. The flower paintings are as much about pure color—sometimes riotous, sometimes almost purely monochromatic—as they are about subject matter. In the 1930s, O'Keeffe wrote about the *White Flower*, 1929 (Plate 67):

Whether the flower or the color is the focus I do not know. I do know that
the flower is painted large to convey to you my experience of the flower—
and what is my experience of the flower—if it is not color.[5]

Her friend, the painter Charles Demuth, described O'Keeffe's color sense in the
brochure accompanying her 1927 exhibit at The Intimate Gallery:

Flowers and flames. And colour. Colour as colour, not as volume, or light,—
only as colour. The last mad throb of red just as it turns green, the
ultimate shriek of orange calling upon all the blues of heaven for relief
or for support; these Georgia O'Keeffe is able to use. In her canvases each
colour almost regains the fun it must have felt within itself, on forming the
first rain-bow.

A great hubbub arose among the public and the critics about the connotations
of the flower paintings. Many found them to be unabashedly sensual, in some cases
overtly erotic. Others perceived them as spiritually chaste. There are stories of parents
who used O'Keeffe's flowers to teach their children about the birds and the bees; and
there are tales of clergy who revered her calla lilies as portrayals in paint of the Immac-
ulate Conception, leading Stieglitz to proclaim O'Keeffe's art as "the beginning of a
new religion."[6] But on the subject of sex and religion in these works, one must draw
one's own conclusions.

Added to the shock of their spectacular size, outrageous color, and scandalous
(or sacred) shapes was the fact that these paintings had been created by a woman at a
time when the art world was almost exclusively male. O'Keeffe had already attracted
attention in the two earlier exhibits of her work at *291*, and in Stieglitz's composite
photographic portrait of her, including many nudes, first shown in 1921. The flower
paintings further fueled the public's fascination with this woman who so freely exposed
herself, and yet retained so much mystery. They were extraordinarily controversial
and sought-after, and made their maker a celebrity. It was the flowers that begat the
O'Keeffe legend in the heady climate of the 1920s.

O'Keeffe had the great daring to lay herself bare, literally and figuratively, at this time in her art and in her life. Stieglitz was right when he said, "O'Keeffe let herself be seen, gave herself like a flower and for an American woman that was too remarkable."[7] And it proved too much for her; the extraordinary self-revelation of these years was contrasted later on by an equally fierce demand for privacy and solitude.

In the summer of 1929, O'Keeffe made a trip to New Mexico, and though she completed several great paintings of flowers there, it was the desert landscape that entranced her. Her first paintings of bones, which symbolized the desert for her, date from 1930, and were combined with flowers. She shipped back East a big wooden barrel full of bones and animal skulls, their crevices stuffed with the calico flowers which Hispanic people of the Southwest used to ornament graves. In the summer of 1931, back at Lake George, she recalled in later years, "I was looking through them one day when someone came to the kitchen door. As I went to answer the door, I stuck a pink rose in the eye socket of a horse's skull. And when I came back the rose in the eye looked pretty fine, so I thought I would just go on with that."[8] That same year, she did go on to *Cow's Skull with Calico Roses*, 1931 (Plate 100), which incorporated the fabric flowers from her extraordinary works *The White Calico Flower*, 1931 (Plate 98) and *White Rose, New Mexico*, 1930 (Plate 99). These paintings marked a turning point in O'Keeffe's life. After this time, she spent much of the year in New Mexico, apart from Stieglitz, and the desert replaced flowers as her primary motif.

It must have been a great relief for her to paint in the desert, in respite from the storm of attention that always seemed to surround her in New York. She could focus on a subject that was close to her heart, yet one that was freed from all of the readings that people had brought to her flowers. "A red hill doesn't touch everyone's heart as it touches mine . . . You have no associations with those hills—our waste land—I think our most beautiful country—You may not have seen it, so you want me always to paint flowers."[9] The New Mexico landscape was to remain an inexhaustible source of inspiration and refuge to her for the rest of her life. She loved the desert precisely because "it is vast and empty and untouchable—and knows no kindness with all its beauty."[10]

I am neither an art historian nor a writer, but I have been an admirer of Georgia O'Keeffe's work for fifteen years. O'Keeffe's flower paintings are so little-known today partly because they were so popular sixty years ago. They consistently sold better than her paintings of other subjects and thus became her signature work. Some entered museum collections, and some were retained by the artist, but most were purchased by private collectors, who kept them or passed them along to family or friends. Over the past half century they have become so widely scattered, and in some cases so well hidden, that the mission of finding them often made me feel more like an archaeologist and private eye than a publisher. For me and my colleagues, the task of assembling them took on the fascination of a hunt for lost treasure. Finding flowers became a delightful obsession.

This book is not definitive, but we hope that it offers a representative selection of this particular aspect of O'Keeffe's vast and monumental achievement. We spent many thousands of hours combing libraries, museums, and archives, tracing the Byzantine lineage of these works across several generations. Usually we began with a reference to a painting found in a letter, exhibition list, article, or catalogue. Sometimes we had no more to work with than a title (often shared by ten other paintings), date (often incorrectly listed), and perhaps the name of a collector who purchased it in 1924, with no address or other information of any kind. We offer our thanks to the myriad collectors, museum curators, gallery owners, family genealogists, and doormen we ruthlessly pestered for clues.

In the course of our research, I've heard many "flower stories" and met many extraordinary people. One of my favorite images is of the collector in her mid-nineties who has treasured a small, jewel-like O'Keeffe flower since she purchased it in the 1920s from Alfred Stieglitz. I am told that she wakes late each morning and walks straight past her Picassos and Matisses to sit for much of the day admiring her O'Keeffe.

One woman told me that her O'Keeffe painting of a petunia was a gift to her from her mother on the day she was born, so that "she would begin life in the right way."

Another work was sold in the 1930s by Alfred Stieglitz to a young woman who very much admired O'Keeffe. He showed her a selection of paintings, and she chose a tiny rosebud. Stieglitz then disappeared into the back room at An American Place and returned with one of his abstract cloud photographs, known as *Equivalents*. He gave it to her on the condition that the two works would always remain side by side. And they have.

A few months ago, as our project neared completion, I realized that I began this book unwittingly the day I first met Georgia O'Keeffe. It was in June 1973, and I was a student in fine arts at Harvard College. I was interested in the work of Stieglitz, and, through his portraits of O'Keeffe, became enamored of her paintings and her personality. The day before graduation one of my art professors told me it was rumored that O'Keeffe would receive an honorary degree from the University the next day. I was awestruck; it had never occurred to me that I might one day have the chance to see in person the extraordinary face and profile that had been immortalized by Stieglitz.

The next morning, I went to the florist in Harvard Square and bought my favorite flower, a giant white peony. I ran into the Yard as the ceremony began, and joined the crowds lining the path of the procession. When O'Keeffe filed past, I stepped out and handed her the flower, saying, "This is for you, Miss O'Keeffe." Without missing a step, and without turning her head to the side, she firmly grasped the flower in her hand, and continued on without speaking.

When I gave Miss O'Keeffe that peony on a late spring day nearly fifteen years ago I had no inkling of how grand and glorious was the bouquet that she would render. As I see these blossoms arrayed before me, I know that no one ever has nor ever will paint flowers the way that Georgia O'Keeffe did, for one simple reason. To paraphrase what she published about Stieglitz in 1978, O'Keeffe's eye was in her, and that way she was always painting herself.[11]

These works of art are the self-portrait of a woman and of an artist in full bloom. They are extraordinary *because* of the complexity and richness of their intimations. They speak of many things—"the idea of filling a space in a beautiful way,"[12] the sheer joy of painting well, one woman's life. To me they are above all the most sublime expression of love that has ever been put into paint.

N.C. · Kyoto, Japan · April 1987

Notes

1. Laurie Lisle, *Portrait of an Artist: A Biography of Georgia O'Keeffe* (New York: Seaview Books, 1980), 137.

2. Ibid.

3. Ibid.

4. Mary Braggiotti, "Her Worlds Are Many," *New York Post*, May 16, 1946.

5. William M. Milliken, "White Flower by Georgia O'Keeffe," *Bulletin of the Cleveland Museum of Art*, April 1937.

6. Herbert J. Seligmann, *Alfred Stieglitz Talking* (New Haven: Yale University Library, 1966), 41.

7. Seligmann, 71.

8. Calvin Tomkins, "The Rose in the Eye Looked Pretty Fine," *New Yorker*, March 4, 1974, 50.

9. Excerpted from the text entitled "About Myself," published in the catalogue accompanying O'Keeffe's 1939 exhibition at An American Place, New York.

10. Ibid.

11. From her preface to *Georgia O'Keeffe: A Portrait by Alfred Stieglitz* (New York: The Metropolitan Museum of Art/The Viking Press, 1978).

12. Georgia O'Keeffe, *Georgia O'Keeffe* (New York: The Viking Press, 1976), opposite Plate 11.

List of Plates

1 *Red Poppy*, 1927
Oil on canvas
7⅛ x 9 inches (18.1 x 22.9 cm)
Private Collection

2 *Black Iris*, 1926
[*The Dark Iris No. III*, 1926]
Oil on canvas
36 x 29⅞ inches (91.4 x 75.9 cm)
The Metropolitan Museum of Art
Alfred Stieglitz Collection, 1969
NY Courtesy Estate of Georgia O'Keeffe

3 *Red Canna*, c. 1919
Watercolor on paper
19⅜ x 13 inches (49.2 x 33 cm)
Yale University Art Gallery
Gift of George Hopper Fitch, B.A.
1932, and Mrs. Fitch

4 *Red Flower*, c. 1918–1919
Oil on canvas
20 x 17 inches (50.8 x 43.2 cm)
The Warner Collection of
Gulf States Paper Corporation
AL Tuscaloosa, Alabama
Courtesy Estate of Georgia O'Keeffe

5 *Red Canna*, 1919
Oil on board
12 x 8⅜ inches (30.5 x 21.3 cm)
Private Collection
PA Courtesy Jeffrey Fuller
Fine Art, Philadelphia

6 *Red Canna*, c. 1919
Oil on board
12 x 9 inches (30.5 x 22.9 cm)
Private Collection

7 *Inside Red Canna*, 1919
Oil on canvas
22 x 17 inches (55.9 x 43.2 cm)
Collection of Michael J. Scharf

8 *Zinnias*, c. 1920
Oil on canvas
12 x 9 inches (30.5 x 22.9 cm)
Courtesy Richard T. York,
New York

9 [*Still Life–Zinnias*], c. 1920
Watercolor on paper
11½ x 8¼ inches (29.2 x 21 cm)
Private Collection

10 *Red Canna*, 1923
Oil on canvas
12 x 9⅞ inches (30.5 x 25.1 cm)
Collection of Mr. and Mrs.
Meyer P. Potamkin

11 *Red Snapdragons*, c. 1923
Oil on canvas
20¼ x 10¼ inches (51.4 x 26 cm)
Private Collection

12 *Petunia No. 2*, 1924
Oil on canvas
36 x 30 inches (91.4 x 76.2 cm)
Estate of Anita O'Keeffe Young

13 *Petunia and Coleus*, 1924
Oil on canvas
36 x 30 inches (91.4 x 76.2 cm)
Private Collection
NY Courtesy Washburn Gallery,
New York

14 *Flower Abstraction*, 1924
Oil on canvas
48 x 30 inches (121.9 x 76.2 cm)
Whitney Museum of American Art
Gift of Sandra Payson
DC Courtesy Estate of Georgia O'Keeffe

15 *Red Canna*, c. 1924
Oil on canvas mounted on masonite
36 x 29⅞ inches (91.4 x 75.9 cm)
University of Arizona Museum of Art
AZ Gift of Oliver James

16 *Purple Petunia*, c. 1925
Oil on canvas
7³⁄₁₆ x 7⅛ inches (18.3 x 18.1 cm)
Private Collection

17 *Red Canna*, 1925
Oil on canvas
29 x 18 inches (73.7 x 45.7 cm)
Private Collection

18 *Petunia, Lake George*, 1925
Oil on board
9⅞ x 6¾ inches (25.1 x 17.1 cm)
Private Collection

19 *Petunia*, 1925
Oil on board
10 x 7 inches (25.4 x 17.8 cm)
Private Collection

20 *Purple Petunias*, 1925
Oil on canvas
NJ 15⅞ x 13 inches (40.3 x 33 cm)
The Newark Museum

21 *Petunia*, 1925
Oil on canvas
17¾ x 21¾ inches (45.1 x 55.2 cm)
Courtesy Kennedy Galleries,
NY New York

22 *Bleeding-Heart*, c. 1928
Oil on board
13½ x 11½ inches (34.3 x 29.2 cm)
Private Collection

23 *Blue Flower*, 1924–28
Oil on board
12¾ x 9½ inches (32.4 x 24.1 cm)
Private Collection
Courtesy Mickelson Gallery,
DC Washington, D.C.

24 *Yellow Sweet Peas*, 1925
Pastel on paper
26½ x 19¼ inches (67.3 x 48.9 cm)
Courtesy Kennedy Galleries,
NY New York

25 *White Sweet Peas*, 1926
Pastel on paper
25 x 18¾ inches (63.5 x 47.6 cm)
Collection of Loretta and
Robert K. Lifton

26 *Pink Sweet Peas*, 1927
Pastel on paper
27½ x 21¾ inches (69.8 x 55.2 cm)
Private Collection

27 *Purple Petunia*, 1927
Oil on canvas
36 x 30 inches (91.4 x 76.2 cm)
Collection of Mr. and Mrs.
Graham Gund

28 *Abstraction—77*, 1925
[*Pink Tulip*, 1925]
Oil on canvas
32 x 12 inches (81.3 x 30.5 cm)
Collection of Emily Fisher Landau,
New York
Courtesy Estate of Georgia O'Keeffe

29 *Pink Tulip*, 1926
Oil on canvas
36 x 30 inches (91.4 x 76.2 cm)
The Baltimore Museum of Art
Bequest of Mabel Garrison Siemonn
In Memory of her Husband,
MR George Siemonn

30 *Black and Purple Petunias*, 1925
Oil on board
20 x 25 inches (50.8 x 63.5 cm)
Private Collection Courtesy Doris Bry
Courtesy Estate of Georgia O'Keeffe

31 *White Iris*, c. 1926
Oil on canvas
24 x 20 inches (61 x 50.8 cm)
Collection of Emily Fisher Landau,
New York
Courtesy Estate of Georgia O'Keeffe

32 *Iris*, 1929
[*Dark Iris No. 2*, 1927]
Oil on canvas
32 x 12 inches (81.3 x 30.5 cm)
Colorado Springs Fine Arts Center
CO Anonymous Gift

33 *The Dark Iris No. II*, 1926
Oil on canvas
9 x 7 inches (22.9 x 17.8 cm)
Private Collection
Courtesy Washburn Gallery,
NY New York

34 *Black Iris II*, 1936
[*Black Iris VI*, 1936]
Oil on canvas
36 x 24 inches (91.4 x 61 cm)
Private Collection

35 *Pansy*, 1926
[*Black Pansy &*
Forget-Me-Nots, 1926]
Oil on canvas
26¹⁵⁄₁₆ x 12¹⁄₁₆ inches (68.4 x 30.6 cm)
The Brooklyn Museum
NY Gift of Mrs. Alfred S. Rossin

36 *Nicotina* [*Nicotiana*], c. 1926
[*Autumn Leaf and White Flower*,
c. 1926]
Oil on canvas
20 x 9 inches (50.8 x 22.9 cm)
Private Collection

37 *Black Petunia & White*
Morning-Glory I, 1926
Oil on canvas
36 x 30 inches (91.4 x 76.2 cm)
Collection of Jean M. Wallace

38 *Black Petunia & White*
Morning-Glory II, 1926
Oil on canvas
36 x 30 inches (91.4 x 76.2 cm)
Private Collection

39 *Morning-Glory with Black*, 1926
[*Black Petunia & White*
Morning-Glory III, 1926]
Oil on canvas
36 x 30 inches (91.4 x 76.2 cm)
The Cleveland Museum of Art
OH Bequest of Leonard C. Hanna, Jr.

40 *Abstraction—White Rose No. 2*, 1927
Oil on canvas
36 x 30 inches (91.4 x 76.2 cm)
Copyright © 1987 Estate of
Georgia O'Keeffe

41 *Abstraction–White Rose No. 3*, 1927
[*Ballet Skirt* or *Electric Light*, 1927]
Oil on canvas
36 x 30 inches (91.4 x 76.2 cm)
Copyright © 1987 Estate of
Georgia O'Keeffe

42 *White Rose with
Larkspur No. 1*, 1927
Oil on canvas
36 x 30 inches (91.4 x 76.2 cm)
Private Collection

43 *White Rose with
Larkspur No. 2*, 1927
Oil on canvas
40 x 30 inches (101.6 x 76.2 cm)
Henry H. and
Zoe Oliver Sherman Fund
Museum of Fine Arts, Boston
MA Courtesy Estate of Georgia O'Keeffe

44 *White Pansy*, 1927
[*Pansy with Forget-Me-Nots*, 1927]
Oil on canvas
36⅛ x 30⅛ inches (91.8 x 76.5 cm)
Copyright © 1987 Estate of
Georgia O'Keeffe

45 *Red Cannas*, 1927
Oil on canvas
36⅛ x 30⅛ inches (91.8 x 76.5 cm)
TX Amon Carter Museum, Fort Worth

46 *Poppy*, 1927
Oil on canvas
30 x 36 inches (76.2 x 91.4 cm)
Museum of Fine Arts
FLA St. Petersburg, Florida

47 *Single Lily with Red*, 1928
[*Calla Lily on Red*, 1928]
Oil on wood
12 x 6¼ inches (30.5 x 15.9 cm)
Whitney Museum
DC of American Art

48 *Calla Lily with
Red Background*, 1923
Oil on board
8⁹⁄₁₆ x 6⁹⁄₁₆ inches (21.7 x 16.7 cm)
Private Collection

49 *Calla Lily*, 1923
Oil on board
12 x 9 inches (30.5 x 22.9 cm)
Private Collection

50 *Calla Lilies*, 1923
Oil on board
32 x 12 inches (81.3 x 30.5 cm)
Private Collection

51 *Lily–Yellow No. 2*, 1927
Oil on canvas
20 x 9 inches (50.8 x 22.9 cm)
The Gerald Peters Gallery, Santa Fe

52 *Yellow Calla*, 1926
Oil on fiberboard
9⅜ x 12¾ inches (23.8 x 32.4 cm)
National Museum of American Art
DC Smithsonian Institution
Gift of the Woodward Foundation

53 *Yellow Calla–Green Leaves*, 1927
[*Lily–Yellow No. 1*, 1927]
Oil on canvas
42 x 16 inches (106.7 x 40.6 cm)
Collection of Mr. Steve Martin

54 *Calla Lily on Grey*, 1928
Oil on canvas
32 x 17 inches (81.3 x 43.2 cm)
The William H. Lane Foundation

55 *Calla Lily with Red Roses*, 1926
[*L.K.–White Calla & Roses*, 1926]
Oil on canvas
30 x 48 inches (76.2 x 121.9 cm)
Private Collection

56 *Calla Lilies with Red Anemone*,
1928
Oil on wood
30 x 48 inches (76.2 x 121.9 cm)
Private Collection

57 *Two Calla Lilies on Pink*, 1928
Oil on canvas
40 x 30 inches (101.6 x 76.2 cm)
Copyright © 1987 Estate of
Georgia O'Keeffe

58 *Pink Rose*, 1928
Oil on canvas
12 x 5¾ inches (30.5 x 14.6 cm)
Private Collection

59 *White Rose*, 1928
[*A Rose on Blue*, 1928]
Oil on canvas
11 x 7 inches (27.9 x 17.8 cm)
Private Collection

60 *Jack-in-the-Pulpit No. 1*, 1930
Oil on canvas
12 x 9 inches (30.5 x 22.9 cm)
NY Private Collection
Courtesy ACA Galleries, New York

61 *Yellow Hickory Leaves
with Daisy*, 1928
Oil on canvas
29⅞ x 39⅞ inches (76 x 101.3 cm)
Gift of Georgia O'Keeffe to the
Alfred Stieglitz Collection
Copyright © 1987
CHGO The Art Institute of Chicago
All Rights Reserved

62 *Jack-in-the-Pulpit No. 2*, 1930
Oil on canvas
40 x 30 inches (101.6 x 76.2 cm)
Copyright © 1987 Estate of
Georgia O'Keeffe

63 *Jack-in-the-Pulpit No. 3*, 1930
Oil on canvas
40 x 30 inches (101.6 x 76.2 cm)
Copyright © 1987 Estate of
Georgia O'Keeffe

64 *Jack-in-the-Pulpit No. 4*, 1930
Oil on canvas
40 x 30 inches (101.6 x 76.2 cm)
Copyright © 1987 Estate of
Georgia O'Keeffe

65 *Jack-in-the-Pulpit No. 5*, 1930
Oil on canvas
48 x 30 inches (121.9 x 76.2 cm)
Copyright © 1987 Estate of
Georgia O'Keeffe

66 *Jack-in-the-Pulpit No. 6*, 1930
Oil on canvas
36 x 18 inches (91.4 x 45.7 cm)
Copyright © 1987 Estate of
Georgia O'Keeffe

67 *White Flower*, 1929
Oil on canvas
30⅛ x 36⅛ inches
(76.5 x 91.8 cm)
The Cleveland Museum of Art
OH Purchased for the
Hinman B. Hurlbut Collection

68 *Red Poppy No. VI*, 1928
Oil on canvas
36 x 30 inches (91.4 x 76.2 cm)
Collection of Reed College

69 *Black Hollyhock,
Blue Larkspur*, 1929
Oil on canvas
36 x 30 inches (91.4 x 76.2 cm)
The Metropolitan Museum of Art
NY George A. Hearn Fund, 1934
Courtesy Estate of Georgia O'Keeffe

70 *Black Hollyhock,
Blue Larkspur*, 1929
Oil on canvas
30 x 40 inches (76.2 x 101.6 cm)
Estate of Anita O'Keeffe Young

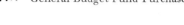

71 *Oriental Poppies*, 1928
[*Red Poppies*, 1928]
Oil on canvas
30 x 40⅛ inches (76.2 x 101.9 cm)
University Art Museum, University
MN of Minnesota, Minneapolis
General Budget Fund Purchase

72 *Yellow Cactus Flowers*, 1929
Oil on canvas
30³⁄₁₆ x 42 inches (76.7 x 106.7 cm)
The Fort Worth Art Museum
Gift of the William E. Scott
TX Foundation

73 *Light Iris*, 1930
[*White Iris*, 1930]
Oil on canvas
40 x 30 inches (101.6 x 76.2 cm)
Virginia Museum of Fine Arts
VA Gift of Mr. and Mrs. Bruce Gottwald

74 *Banana Flower No. 1*, 1933
Charcoal on paper
22 x 15 inches (55.9 x 38.1 cm)
The Arkansas Art Center Foundation
Collection
AK The Museum Purchase Plan of the
N.E.A. and the Tabriz Fund, 1974

75 *Banana Plant No. 4*, 1933
Charcoal on paper
21½ x 14⅜ inches (54.6 x 36.5 cm)
Private Collection

76 *Banana Flower*, 1933
Charcoal on paper
21¾ x 14¾ inches (55.2 x 37.5 cm)
Gift to American Association of
University Women from
Mary Alice Parrish, Ph.D., Vandalia,
Missouri

77 *Banana Flower*, 1933
Charcoal on paper
21¾ x 14¾ inches (55.2 x 37.5 cm)
Collection, The Museum of Modern Art,
NY New York
Given Anonymously (by exchange)

78 *Calla Lilies*, 1930
Oil on canvas
15 x 12½ inches (38.1 x 31.7 cm)
LA The Davis Family Fund, on loan to
the New Orleans Museum of Art

79 *Bleeding-Heart*, 1932
Pastel on paper
15 x 10 inches (38.1 x 25.4 cm)
Estate of Anita O'Keeffe Young

80 *Spotted Lily*, 1935
Watercolor and pencil on paper
15¼ x 12½ inches (38.7 x 31.7 cm)
Courtesy Hirschl & Adler Galleries,
NY New York/The Gerald Peters Gallery,
Santa Fe

81 *Pink Roses and Larkspur*, 1931
Pastel on paper
16 x 12 inches (40.6 x 30.5 cm)
Private Collection
Courtesy Doris Bry, New York

82 *Lilac, Carnation, Tulip*, 1938
[*Flowers, 1941*]
Oil on board
13⅜ x 8½ inches (34 x 21.6 cm)
Collection of Olga Hirshhorn,
Washington, D.C.

83 *Apple Blossoms*, 1930
Oil on canvas
37 x 26 inches (94 x 66 cm)
The Nelson-Atkins Museum of Art
Kansas City, Missouri
MO Gift of Mrs. Louis Sosland

84 *Red Amaryllis*, 1937
Oil on canvas
11⅞ x 10 inches (30.2 x 25.4 cm)
Terra Museum of American Art,
Chicago, Illinois
CHGO Gift of Mrs. Henrietta Roig,
Winnetka, Illinois

85 *Sunflower, New Mexico, II*, 1935
Oil on canvas
19 x 13 inches (48.3 x 33 cm)
Collection of Kay and Warner LeRoy

86 *Mountain Flowers,
Mariposa Lily*, 1940
Oil on canvas
14 x 10 inches (35.6 x 25.4 cm)
Private Collection
Courtesy Richard York Gallery,
New York
NY

87 *Cup of Silver*, 1939
Oil on canvas
19⁹⁄₁₆ x 16⅛ inches (48.7 x 41 cm)
The Baltimore Museum of Art
MD Gift of Cary Ross

88 *Two Jimson Weeds*, 1939
Oil on canvas
36 x 30 inches (91.4 x 76.2 cm)
Estate of Anita O'Keeffe Young

89 *The Miracle Flower*, 1936
Oil on linen
72 x 84 inches (182.9 x 213.4 cm)
Collection of Elizabeth Arden, Inc.

90 *White Primrose*, 1947
Oil on canvas
26 x 20 inches (66 x 50.8 cm)
Private Collection

91 *White Flower on
Red Earth No. 1*, 1943
Oil on canvas
26 x 30¼ inches (66 x 76.8 cm)
NJ The Newark Museum

92 *Narcissa's Last Orchid*, 1941
Pastel on paper
21½ x 27¼ inches (54.5 x 69.1 cm)
The Art Museum,
Princeton University
NJ Gift of David H. McAlpin

93 *White Camellia*, 1938
Pastel on paper
20⅝ x 27⅜ inches (52.4 x 69.5 cm) *OC*
Private Collection

94 *An Orchid*, 1941
Pastel on paper
27 x 21 inches (68.6 x 53.3 cm)
Copyright © 1987 Estate of
Georgia O'Keeffe

95 *Poppies*, 1950
Oil on canvas
36 x 30 inches (91.4 x 76.2 cm)
Milwaukee Art Museum
WI Gift of Mrs. Harry Lynde Bradley

96 *Jimson Weed*, 1932
Oil on canvas
48 x 40 inches (121.9 x 101.6 cm)
Estate of Anita O'Keeffe Young

97 *The White Trumpet Flower*, 1932
Oil on canvas
30 x 40 inches (76.2 x 101.6 cm)
San Diego Museum of Art
Donor Mrs. Inez Grant Parker
In Memory of Earle W. Grant

98 *The White Calico Flower*, 1931
Oil on canvas
30 x 36 inches (76.2 x 91.4 cm)
DC Whitney Museum of American Art

99 *White Rose, New Mexico*, 1930
Oil on canvas
30 x 36 inches (76.2 x 91.4 cm)
Private Collection

100 *Cow's Skull with
Calico Roses*, 1931
Oil on canvas
35⅞ x 24 inches (91.2 x 61 cm)
Gift of Georgia O'Keeffe
Copyright © 1987
The Art Institute of Chicago
All Rights Reserved
CHGO

*List of Plates compiled by
Alexandra Arrowsmith.*

Notes

Steven Sloman was especially commissioned to make the 8 x 10 inch color transparencies for this book. All color photography is by Mr. Sloman, except for the following plates: Kerry Dundas, 72; Gregory Heins, courtesy Art Resource, New York, 27; L. Lorenz, 45; Alan Newman, 84, 95; Robert Reck, 15; Trevor Roehl, 74; Joseph Szaszfai, 3; Malcolm Varon, 2, 28, 31, 69 all Copyright © Malcolm Varon; Art Institute of Chicago, 61, 100; Museum of Fine Arts, Boston, 43, 54; courtesy Gulf States Paper Corporation, 4; courtesy James Maroney, 53; Museum of Modern Art, New York, 77; Gerald Peters Gallery, 51.

In the List of Plates, dimensions of paintings are given in inches and centimeters, height preceding width. Measurements have been rounded to the nearest sixteenth of an inch, and to the nearest millimeter. Title, date, medium, and dimension have been determined by consulting and crosschecking the following sources: the painting itself, including any information on the back; the institution or collector who owns the work; the American Art Research Council O'Keeffe archive, compiled by Rosalind Irvine and Doris Bry, at the Whitney Museum of American Art Library, New York; The Downtown Gallery Papers at the Archives of American Art, New York; The Stieglitz Archive in the Collection of American Literature at the Beinecke Rare Book and Manuscript Library, Yale University; the libraries of the Museum of Modern Art, New York, and the Department of 20th Century Art at the Metropolitan Museum of Art, New York; checklists and installation photographs from exhibitions at *291*, Anderson Galleries, The Intimate Gallery, An American Place, and The Downtown Gallery; and catalogues of other exhibitions held of O'Keeffe's work in galleries and museums.

In many instances more than one title and date exist for a painting. When alternate titles have been found in our research this has been noted in square brackets. If there is a discrepancy in the date of a work, we have so indicated in the catalogue entry by placing a "c." (circa) before the date that has been determined to be the most likely.

A number of these works have been exhibited and published both horizontally and vertically. O'Keeffe and Stieglitz stated that certain paintings could be viewed in different directions, and at times they even indicated this on the back of the canvas.

In all cases the paintings are reproduced in their entirety.

Acknowledgements

My great thanks are given to all those listed below, and to the many museums, private collectors, galleries, and more, without whose generous assistance this publication would not have been possible. I am most grateful to several individuals who have shaped this book: Kate Giel and Sandy Arrowsmith, Associate Editors; Steven Sloman, photographer; Doris Bry, authority on the life and work of Georgia O'Keeffe; P. J. Collins, Hiroyuki Nakao, and all of the extraordinary craftsmen of Nissha Printing Company. Your combined talents and your tireless pursuit of perfection are eloquently displayed on these pages.

N. C.

Anne Adams
Amon Carter Museum, Fort Worth

Jean Addison
The Cleveland Museum of Art

Neale M. Albert, Esq.
Paul, Weiss, Rifkind, Wharton & Garrison, New York

Rachel M. Allen
National Museum of American Art, Washington, DC

Dick Amt
National Gallery of Art, Washington, DC

Hideo Aoki
Motovun Tokyo

Pierre Apraxine
Gilman Paper Company, New York

Art & Commerce
New York, NY

James K. Ballinger
Phoenix Art Museum

Loraine Baratti
Whitney Museum of American Art, New York

Ira Bartfield
National Gallery of Art, Washington, DC

Jane Bay
LucasFilm, San Rafael, CA

Melissa Bellinelli
James Maroney, Inc., New York

John Benson
Letterer and Stone Carver

Richard Benson
Photographer and Printer

Sidney L. Bergen
ACA Galleries, New York

John Berggruen
John Berggruen Gallery, San Francisco

Peter Bermingham
University of Arizona Museum of Art, Tucson

Lynn Bettmann
Kennedy Galleries, New York

Peter Biasotti
Photo Marketplace, New York

Marcia Bickoff
Beinecke Rare Book and Manuscript Library, New Haven

Bill Blades
Sotheby Parke-Bernet, New York

Dominick Blasi
The Brooklyn Museum

Dr. Karl H. Blessing
Droemer Knaur Verlag, Munich, Germany

Paul E. Bragdon
Reed College, Portland, OR

Fred Brandt
Virginia Museum of Fine Arts, Richmond

Lillian Brenwasser
Kennedy Galleries, New York

Steven Brezzo
San Diego Museum of Art

Susan Brown
University of Minnesota Art Museum, Minneapolis

Louise Brownell
Terra Museum of American Art, Evanston, IL

Arlene P. Bruhn
American Association of University Women, Washington, DC

Dr. Anne L. Bryant
American Association of University Women, Washington, DC

E. John Bullard
New Orleans Museum of Art

Peter C. Bunnell
The Art Museum, Princeton University

Elizabeth Cabana
Franchini+Cabana, Inc., New York

Ely Reeves Callaway, Jr.
Callaway Hickory Stick USA, Carlsbad, CA

Ely Reeves Callaway III
Callaway Cars, Lyme, CT

E. A. Carmean, Jr.
The Fort Worth Art Museum

Jamie Carse
Musician

Joanne Cassullo
Washburn Gallery, New York

May Castleberry
Whitney Museum of American Art, New York

Cisley Celmer
Milwaukee Art Museum

Charles Chamot
Artist

Gary Chassman
Chassman & Bem Booksellers, Burlington, VT

Bert Clarke
Book Designer and Typographer

Angela Clauson
American-Australian Foundation for the Arts, Houston, TX

Marthi Cobb
Reed College, Portland, OR

Mo Cohen
Gingko Press, Hamburg, Germany

Joan B. Collins
Richard York Gallery, New York

Conservation Staff
National Museum of American Art, Washington, DC

Mariana Cook
Photographer

Helen Cooper
Yale University Art Gallery, New Haven

James Cornelius
Writer

Deborah Emont Cott
The Nelson-Atkins Museum of Art, Kansas City, MO

Deanna Cross
Metropolitan Museum of Art, New York

William Cuffe
Yale University Art Gallery, New Haven

Yolanda Cuomo
Designer

Harold Daitch, Esq.
Estate of Alexander Calder

Paul Davis
Saint Joseph College, West Hartford, CT

Evan R. Dawson, Esq.
Estate of Anita O'Keeffe Young

Dolores D. Deck
Estate of Anita O'Keeffe Young

Patricia Denson
Gerald Peters Gallery, Santa Fe

Kenneth Deroux
Alaska State Museum, Juneau

James DeYoung
Milwaukee Art Museum

Ben Diep
Hong Color Lab, New York

Ernie Dieringer
Catharine Cooke Studio, Inc., New York

John Dinklemeyer
Sotheby Parke-Bernet, New York

Margaret C. DiSalvi
The Newark Museum

Susan d'Laet
Quebec, Canada

Minoru Terada Domberger
Director & Producer

Edward Downe
Publisher

Diane Driessen
Milwaukee Art Museum

Anita Duquette
Whitney Museum of American Art, New York

Dr. Charles C. Eldredge III
National Museum of American Art, Washington, DC

John Emmerling
Photographer

Lee Ewing
Natural History Magazine, New York

Danny Ferrington
Luthier

James L. Fisher
The Fort Worth Art Museum

Lawrence A. Fleischman
Kennedy Galleries, New York

Frank P. Florey
Colorado Springs Fine Arts Center

Carol Fonde
Custom Color Printer

Alessandro Franchini
Franchini+Cabana, Inc., New York

Fritz Frauchiger
Contemporary Arts Center, Honolulu

Mary Kay Freedman
National Museum of American Art, Washington, DC

Marcus Frey-Daleo
Graphic Designer

Hideshi Fujimaki
Ann Harakawa Design, New York

Jeffrey Fuller
Jeffrey Fuller Fine Art, Philadelphia

Christopher Fulton
Allentown Art Museum, PA

Donald C. Gallup
Beinecke Rare Book and Manuscript Library, New Haven

Robert Gambone
University of Minnesota Art Museum, Minneapolis

Tom Gessler
Museum of Fine Arts, St. Petersburg, FL

Debra Giel
Medical Editor

Edward & Shirley Giel
Brooklyn Park, MN

Leslie Gliedman
Sotheby Parke-Bernet, New York

Elizabeth Gombosi
Harvard University Art Museum, Cambridge

Jean François Gonthier
Edipresse Publishing Group, Lausanne, Switzerland

Michael Goodison
Smith College Museum of Art, Northampton, MA

Robert A. Gottlieb
The New Yorker

Thomas D. Grischkowsky
Museum of Modern Art, New York

Charles Gurein
Colorado Springs Fine Arts Center

Delbert R. Gutridge
The Cleveland Museum of Art

Margaret Haight
Artist

Suzanne Hall
Virginia Museum of Fine Arts, Richmond

Thom Hall
Arkansas Art Center, Little Rock

Maria Morris Hambourg
Metropolitan Museum of Art, New York

Jemison Hammond
Archives of American Art, New York

Jane Hankins
Museum of Fine Arts, Boston

Robert A. Harman
Pennsylvania Academy of the Fine Arts, Philadelphia

Lewis Harrington
Photographer

Stephen Harvard
Meriden-Stinehour Press, Lunenburg, VT

John H. Hauberg
Seattle, Washington

Simon Haviland
Phaidon Press Ltd., Oxford, England

David Heald
Photographer

Caroline Hicks
Administrative Assistant

Charles Hilburn
Gulf States Paper Corporation, Tuscaloosa, AL

Tom Hinson
The Cleveland Museum of Art

Nicholas Hlobeczy
The Cleveland Museum of Art

Karen C. Hodges
Phoenix Art Museum

Chris Hoffman
Production Assistant

Laura B. Hoge
Colorado Springs Fine Arts Center

Kerry Hoggard
American Association of University Women, Washington, DC

Katy Homans
Homans Design, New York

Angela Hudson
Sotheby Parke-Bernet, New York

Jane Isaacs
Columbus Museum of Art, OH

Eiko Ishioka
Japan's Ultimate Designer

Ben Izett
Assistant to Steven Sloman

Mary Moore Jacoby
Virginia Museum of Fine Arts, Richmond

Bron Janulis
Terra Museum of American Art, Evanston, IL

Nan Jernigan
Publishing Consultant

Mark M. Johnson
Muscarelle Museum of Art, Williamsburg, VA

Patricia M. Jones
Elizabeth Arden, Inc., New York

Louise Lambert Kale
Muscarelle Museum of Art, Williamsburg, VA

Stephanie Karandanis
Fashion Model

Bill Katz
Artist

Patricia Kelleher
Catharine Cooke Studio, Inc., New York

Anne Kennedy
Art & Commerce, New York

Mayumi Kitamura
Assistant to Eiko Ishioka

Barbara Kittle
University of Arizona Museum of Art, Tucson

Barbara Klein
Sotheby Parke-Bernet, New York

Tsunehiro Kobayashi
Photographer

Bob Kolbrener
Photographer

Charlotta Kotik
The Brooklyn Museum

Jim Kraft
Whitney Museum of American Art, New York

Raymond R. Krueger, Esq.
Charne, Glassner, Tehan, Clancy & Taitelman, Milwaukee

Christopher Kuntze
Meriden-Stinehour Press, Meriden, CT

Carmen Lacey
San Diego Museum of Art

William H. Lane
The William H. Lane Foundation, Lunenburg, MA

Margie Laughlin
Museum of Fine Arts, St. Petersburg, FL

Jack W. Laurien
Elizabeth Arden, Inc., New York

Marguerite Lavin
The Brooklyn Museum

Arnold L. Lehman
Baltimore Museum of Art

Diane Lesko
Museum of Fine Arts, St. Petersburg, FL

Gerald Linder
Phoenix Art Museum

Laurie Lisle
Author

Pat Loikow
Museum of Fine Arts, Boston

Tina Lopez
Assistant to Neale M. Albert, Esq.

Joan Lothrop
Northridge, CA

Karen Lovaas
University of Minnesota Art Museum, Minneapolis

Nancy Loving
The Nelson-Atkins Museum of Art, Kansas City, MO

George Lucas
LucasFilm, San Rafael, CA

Pat Maloney
Administrative Assistant

Lee Marks
Gilman Paper Company, New York

James Maroney
James Maroney, Inc., New York

Peter C. Marzio
The Museum of Fine Arts, Houston

Jerry Mathiason
Photographer

Margaret McCarthy
Pennsylvania Academy of the Fine Arts, Philadelphia

David McClelland
Bloomfield Hills, MI

Maureen McCormick
The Art Museum, Princeton University

Katie McDonald
San Francisco, CA

William McNaught
Archives of American Art, New York

Ellen McNeilly
Alfred A. Knopf, Inc., New York

Grete Meilman
Grete Meilman Fine Art, Ltd., New York

Lisa Mintz Messinger
Metropolitan Museum of Art, New York

Sidney S. Mickelson
Mickelson Gallery, Washington, DC

Pat Middleton
Beinecke Rare Book and Manuscript Library, New Haven

Michael Milkovich
Museum of Fine Arts, St. Petersburg, FL

Samuel S. Miller
The Newark Museum

Issey Miyake
Fashion Designer

Jane Montgomery
Harvard University Art Museum, Cambridge

Les Morsillo
Photographer

Keiko Motonaga
Assistant to Eiko Ishioka

Jan K. Muhlert
Amon Carter Museum, Fort Worth

Hansen Mulford
Orlando Museum of Art

James Mundy
Milwaukee Art Museum

Yutaka Murachi
Nissha Printing Company, Ltd., Kyoto

Yasuyuki Murata
Nissha Printing Company, Ltd., Kyoto

Cynthia Nakamura
Denver Art Museum

Jose Naranjo
National Gallery of Art, Washington, DC

M. P. Naud
Hirschl & Adler Galleries, New York

Robert Nelson
Elizabeth Arden, Inc., New York

Scott Newrock
The Typecrafters, Inc., New York

Sabrina O'Meara
Bookbinder

Nathaniel Owings
Owings-Dewey Fine Art, Santa Fe

Doris Palca
Whitney Museum of American Art, New York

Arlene Panca-Graham
Archives of American Art, New York

Irving Penn
Photographer

Paul N. Perrot
Virginia Museum of Fine Arts, Richmond

Gerald P. Peters III
Peters Corporation, Santa Fe

Martin Petersen
San Diego Museum of Art

Paul Piazza
Colorado Springs Fine Arts Center

Dan Piersol
New Orleans Museum of Art

John Poliszuk
Museum Specialist, Washington, DC

Hall Powell
Screenwriter

Nancy Boyle Press
The Baltimore Museum of Art

Genie Priddy
National Museum of American Art, Washington, DC

Sergio Purtell
Photographer

Sharon Queeney
Elizabeth Arden, Inc., New York

Ann Radice
National Museum for Women in the Arts, Washington, DC

Françoise and Harvey Rambach
New York, NY

David Ramchal
U.S. Color Lab, New York

Peter Rathbone
Sotheby Parke-Bernet, New York

Reference Staff
New York Public Library

Jurg Rehbein
Assistant to Steven Sloman

James L. Reinish
Hirschl & Adler Galleries, New York

Barbara Reiss
Metropolitan Museum of Art, New York

David Restad
Phoenix Art Museum

Gary Reynolds
The Newark Museum

Brenda Richardson
The Baltimore Museum of Art

Mr. and Mrs. Harold Rifkin
New York, NY

Joseph Ronchetti
Elizabeth Arden, Inc., New York

Rona Roob
Museum of Modern Art, New York

Marc Rosen
Elizabeth Arden, Inc., New York

Steven Rosen
Columbus Museum of Art

Allen D. Rosenbaum
The Art Museum, Princeton University

Jeremy Ross
Time/Life Books, Alexandria, VA

Elsie Y. Sakuma
The Nelson-Atkins Museum of Art, Kansas City, MO

Christa Sammons
Beinecke Rare Book & Manuscript Library, New Haven

Amy Baker Sandback
ArtForum, New York

Michael Sanden
Terra Museum of American Art, Evanston, IL

Janice Sarkow
Museum of Fine Arts, Boston

Stefano Scafetta
National Museum of American Art, Washington, DC

Ellen Schall
Randolph-Macon Woman's College, Maier Museum of Art, Lynchburg, VA

Terry Schank
Art Institute of Chicago

Kathi Scharer
Assistant to Steven Sloman

E. G. Schempf
The Nelson-Atkins Museum of Art, Kansas City, MO

Victor Schrager
Photographer

Jean Schroeder
Phoenix Art Museum

Rainald Schwarz-Gassner
Droemer Knaur Verlag, Munich, Germany

Roger Sears
Phaidon Press Ltd., Oxford, England

June O'Keeffe Sebring
Kailua, HI

Jeanette Semon
Phoenix Art Museum

Johanna Semple
Swid Powell, New York

Chen Shapira
Assistant to Steven Sloman

Mary Sheridan
Hirschl & Adler Galleries, New York

Don Sigovich
Gamma One Conversions, New York

Patterson Sims
Whitney Museum of American Art, New York

Mimi Sinozich
Terra Museum of American Art, Evanston, IL

James Sly
Computer Consultant

Frances Smyth
National Gallery of Art, Washington, DC

Theodore E. Stebbins
Museum of Fine Arts, Boston

Judy Stein
Pennsylvania Academy of the Fine Arts, Washington, DC

Victoria Stevens
Sudo Tours, New York

Kristy Stewart
Art Institute of Chicago

Stephen R. Stinehour
Meriden-Stinehour Press, Meriden, CT

Stephanie Stitt
National Museum for Women in the Arts, Washington, DC

Connie Sullivan
Polaroid Corporation, Cambridge, MA

Eileen Sullivan
Metropolitan Museum of Art, New York

Mary Suzor
National Gallery of Art, Washington, DC

Hajimu Takemura
Nissha Printing Company, Ltd., Kyoto

Paul J. Tarver
New Orleans Museum of Art

Richard S. Teitz
Denver Art Museum

Daniel Terra
Terra Museum of American Art, Evanston, IL

Liane Thatcher
The Gund Collection, Cambridge, MA

Eugene Thaw
Art Collector

Suzanne Thesing
Collection Thyssen-Bornemisza, Lugano, Switzerland

Vance Thompson
Hirschl & Adler Galleries, New York

Richard L. Tooke
Museum of Modern Art, New York

Jim Tormey
Ann Harakawa Design, New York

Carol Troyen
Museum of Fine Arts, Boston

Barbara Tuchman
Author

Rudy Turk
Arizona State University Art Collections, Tempe

David G. Turner
Museum of Fine Arts, Museum of New Mexico, Santa Fe

Evan Turner
The Cleveland Museum of Art

Vincenza Uccello
Saint Joseph College, West Hartford, CT

U.S. Color Lab
New York, NY

John Van Doren
Gerald Peters Gallery, Santa Fe

Julie von der Roppe
Gingko Press, Hamburg, Germany

Michel Voyski
Artist

Allison E. Wagner
The Fort Worth Art Museum, TX

David W. Wallace, Esq.
Estate of Anita O'Keeffe Young

Jonathan Warner
Gulf States Paper Corporation, Tuscaloosa, AL

Joan Washburn
Washburn Gallery, New York

Harriet M. Watson
Reed College, Portland, OR

Robert Weil
Robert Weil Gallery, Los Angeles

Howard Weingrow
Art Collector

Warren Weitman
Sotheby Parke-Bernet, New York

Jerry Wertheim, Esq.
Jones, Snead, Wertheim, Rodriguez & Wentworth, Santa Fe

David Wharton
Photographer

Eric P. Widing
Richard York Gallery, New York

Mary Jane Williams
Arizona State University Art Collections, Tempe

Mark F. Wilson
The Nelson-Atkins Museum of Art, Kansas City, MO

Amy Wolf
ACA Galleries, New York

Townsend Wolfe
The Arkansas Art Center, Little Rock

James Wood
Art Institute of Chicago

L. Anthony Wright, Jr.
Denver Art Museum

Sadaharu Yamashita
Nissha Printing Company, Ltd., Kyoto

Floyd Yearout
Book Producer and Publisher

Richard T. York
Richard York Gallery, New York

Françoise Zimmerli
Edipresse Publishing Group, Lausanne, Switzerland

Colophon

This book has been researched, edited, designed, and produced by Callaway Editions under the direction of Nicholas Callaway.
Kathleen Giel was Associate Editor and Project Coordinator. Alexandra Arrowsmith was Associate Editor and Research Coordinator.
Susan Ralston was Editor at Alfred A. Knopf.
Jane Friedman and Jeff Stone supervised the publication of this edition, with assistance from Beth Chang.
All 8 x 10 color photography was made especially for this book by Steven Sloman, New York, unless otherwise noted.
Typographic design, layout, and mechanicals were by Ann Harakawa Design, and by Franchini + Cabana, Inc.
Typographic design, layout, and mechanicals for this edition were by Katy Homans. Caissa Douwes was Production Assistant.
Hand retouching of master transparencies was by Beverly Dieringer of Catharine Cooke Studio, Inc., New York.
The typeface for the text is Monotype Walbaum, a typeface originally cut by J. E. Walbaum (1768–1839).
The type was set by Michael and Winifred Bixler, Skaneateles, New York.
The ornament on the front cover is from a brooch made in 1930 by Alexander Calder for Georgia O'Keeffe.
The signature is in O'Keeffe's hand. The rendering of both is by Julian Waters.

Georgia O'Keeffe: One Hundred Flowers
has been printed and bound in Kyoto, Japan, by Nissha Printing Company, under the direction of Shozo Suzuki.
The plates have been made from 175-line screen separations laser-scanned directly from the master transparencies,
and printed in four-color offset lithography on 157 GSM New Age paper.
The book has been smyth-sewn in eight-page signatures. The jacket has been printed in six colors with a matte film lamination.
P. J. Collins was Production Coordinator in New York.
Hiroyuki Nakao was Production Coordinator in Kyoto, with guidance from Masaru Fujimoto,
Managing Director of the International Division, and assistance from Hiroshi Kurosawa.
The Printing Director was Iwao Matsui.
The printing of the book was supervised by Nicholas Callaway and Doris Bry.